8/15

CHALLENGE
YOURSELF

OUTRAGEOUS ANIMALS

WEIRD TRIVIA AND UNBELIEVABLE FACTS TO TEST YOUR KNOWLEDGE
ABOUT MAMMALS, FISH, INSECTS, & MORE!

10/17
Lexile: _____1040L_____

AR/BL: _____

AR Points: _____

D0067352

JEFF PROBST

CHALLENGE YOURSELF

OUTRAGEOUS ANIMALS

Puffin Books
An Imprint of Penguin Group (USA)

PUFFIN BOOKS
Published by the Penguin Group
Penguin Group (USA) LLC
375 Hudson Street
New York, New York 10014

USA * Canada * UK * Ireland * Australia
New Zealand * India * South Africa * China

penguin.com
A Penguin Random House Company

First published in the United States of America by Puffin Books,
an imprint of Penguin Young Readers Group, 2015

Copyright © 2015 by Jeff Probst

Penguin supports copyright. Copyright fuels creativity, encourages diverse voices, promotes
free speech, and creates a vibrant culture. Thank you for buying an
authorized edition of this book and for complying with copyright laws by not reproducing,
scanning, or distributing any part of it in any form without
permission. You are supporting writers and allowing Penguin to
continue to publish books for every reader.

LIBRARY OF CONGRESS CATALOGING-IN-PUBLICATION DATA IS AVAILABLE

Puffin Books Hardcover ISBN 978-0-14-751616-9
Paperback ISBN 978-0-14-751375-5

Printed in China

1 3 5 7 9 10 8 6 4 2

Designed by Maria Fazio

Photo Credits

Thinkstock: Pages i, ii, 6–7, 9, 13, 17, 19–20, 22–26, 29–31, 36–40, 43–44, 46–48, 51–55,
57–58, 60–61, 63–64, 66–67, 70–71, 73–77, 80–81, 83–84, 87–95, 97, 99, 102–103,
106–107, 110, 112–116, 118–119, 121, 124–125, 127–128, 130–131, 133, 135,
138–142, 144–149, 152–159

Shutterstock: Pages vi, 2–5, 7–8, 10, 13–14, 16–18, 22–27, 33–34, 36–37, 42–43, 45,
53, 67, 69, 77–78, 89, 91, 93, 97–99, 101, 105, 108–109, 113–115, 118, 122, 127,
135, 141, 149, 150, 153, 155

iStock: Pages 37, 52, 62, 83, 87, 136, 152–153

All other photos courtesy the author

For Michael and Ava,
I love sharing this adventure with you!

—Dad

Photos this page © Jeff Probst

Hey, young readers!

I really hope you dig this book! We had a lot of fun putting it together.

Survivor has taken me all over the world and I've seen a lot of "outrageous animals," but there are some crazy cool animals in this book that I had never even heard of before!

I hope it inspires a sense of adventure in your soul. It's a big, fun world out there, and one thing I always say to my own kids is, "The adventure you're ready for is the one you get." So go for it every day!

Jeff Probst

Note to readers:
See a word in bold? Check out the glossary in the back to find out what it means!

THE ULTIMATE SPRINTER!

CHEETAH

The fastest land animal, the cheetah can sprint at speeds of more than 62 miles per hour in order to catch gazelles and other smaller hoofed animals. Cheetahs run so fast, in fact, that they steer not with their legs but with their tails, using them like rudders on a boat!

BABY STINGRAY

Have you ever seen the adorable underbellies of baby stingrays? Their nostrils and mouth together form a smiley face. And when they swim upward, their pelvic fins resemble small "dancing" legs.

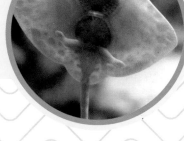

AXOLOTL

Axolotls, or walking fish, aren't truly fish. Also named the Mexican salamander, these amphibians have a comical grin when seen straight on. They're able to regenerate limbs, like a starfish! Unfortunately, axolotls are close to extinction. In 2013, a 4-month-long search uncovered no wild specimens.

CUTTLEFISH

Despite their name, cuttlefish are not fish at all, but mollusks. And they also shouldn't be cuddled with! These close relatives of squid and octopuses are equipped with a **neurotoxin**, a venom that affects how the mind communicates with the body.

PUFFER FISH

Despite their appearance, puffer fish are the second most poisonous vertebrate animal on the planet, second only to the golden dart frog. When threatened, puffer fish quickly inflate like a balloon. If swallowed, the poison of puffer fish causes suffocation. Cute but deadly!

POLAR BEAR

Polar bears weigh as much as 2,200 pounds, making them the world's largest land carnivores. Living near the Arctic Circle, polar bears primarily eat seals. Kodiak brown bears are similar in size, but they are believed to have a less carnivorous diet, eating plants some of the year.

CRAZY BUT TRUE

Polar bears look white, but it's a bit of an optical illusion. The truth is their fur is actually transparent and their skin is black!

SOUTHERN ELEPHANT SEAL

The southern elephant seal is the largest of all carnivores. Weighing an average of 7,000 pounds, a male southern elephant seal is called a bull and eats mostly fish and squid. The largest bull on record weighed an estimated 11,000 pounds!

LEAST WEASEL

The world's smallest carnivore is the least weasel, often fewer than 9 inches long. Despite its small size, it is a surprisingly fierce carnivore, killing and eating half of its own body weight in fresh meat every day—including some larger animals 10 times its own size.

SCORPIONS VS. SPIDERS

SPIDER

Like spiders, scorpions have 8 hairy legs, which they use to feel for vibrations in the ground. Their bodies are divided into 2 segments, and like spiders they molt and grow in size as they age. Also like spiders, scorpions are predatory and venomous, sustaining themselves by killing and eating small animals, usually other insects.

Along with ticks and mites, scorpions are arachnids that inspire fear in people throughout the

WORLD.

Larger than most spiders, a scorpion's body parts are larger, too. While spiders carry venom in relatively small fangs, scorpions have larger pincers, which they use to hold their prey as they inject their venom using a tail stinger. As is true with spiders, some scorpions have dangerously strong venom—though only about 50 out of 1,500 known species of scorpions have venom toxic enough to kill a human.

SCORPION

Photo © Jeff Probst

This mother scorpion I saw in Nicaragua impressed me! Unlike spiders, female scorpions give birth to live young. They even care for their offspring, carrying their children on their backs until the young arachnids are able to care for themselves.

Many years ago we were shooting *Survivor* in Kenya, Africa. One morning I got out of my tent and went to put on my shoes. I forgot to do the most important thing—check them first! There was a scorpion in my shoe, and it stung my foot! It hurt so much I couldn't walk for hours. Their sting is no joke!

BIRDS OF A FEATHER

There are about 10,000 species of birds, and they all have feathers. They also all have wings, a toothless beak, two legs, and a backbone. Birds are all warm-blooded. And they all lay eggs. Well, actually, only the females do.

ORCAS

Also called killer whales, fish tigers, and "wolves of the sea," orcas are not whales at all, but the largest of all dolphins. An adult orca can grow up to 32 feet long and weigh 12,000 pounds, 600 times the size of a grown man.

Just like bats and other dolphins, orcas use a sonar process called **echolocation** to gain a sense of their surroundings. Here's how it works: the orca makes a sound and then waits to hear the echo. The echo is created when the sound bounces off of something else that's swimming in the water. Based on how quickly the orca hears the echo, it has a good idea of how close the potential prey might be!

Groups of 30 or 40 orcas hunt together in **pods**, devouring other dolphins, as well as seals, sea lions, squid, fish, birds, and smaller whales (such as narwhals, beluga, and gray whales). They even eat great white sharks! Working together, orcas gang up on their prey, confusing schools of fish by blowing bubbles or blocking a young whale from surfacing for air.

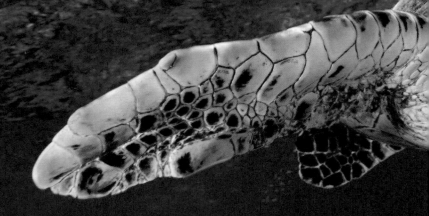

ANCIENT SPECIES!

Sea turtles have been around since the time of the **dinosaurs!**

Though they're perfectly adapted for ocean life, able to stay underwater for hours at a time, sea turtles need oxygen to live. Unlike other turtles, they can't retract their legs and head into their shells to protect themselves. They also are color-blind and don't see very well outside of the water.

SEA TURTLES

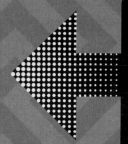

BABY SEA TURTLES MAKING THEIR WAY TO THE WATER

Though they're most comfortable in the ocean, sea turtles reproduce on land. The mother turtles bury their eggs in the sand, sometimes as many as 190 eggs at once. When the eggs hatch, the baby turtles dig themselves out and slowly make their way to the ocean by instinct.

I had an amazing opportunity in Nicaragua last summer to witness turtles laying their eggs. It was so cool! The beach was a protected sanctuary designed to keep them as safe as possible, and my family and I were invited by the owners. Around 10 p.m., I took our kids and their cousins down to the beach, and we sat quietly in the dark and just watched as hundreds of turtles came in from the ocean, crawled ashore, and found their spot on the sandy beach. After about 10 minutes of finding the perfect spot, they finally dug into the sand and began the process of laying eggs. Our expert guide was able to dig a hole in the sand and shine a flashlight into the hole so that we could see the eggs actually dropping into the sand. It was amazing. We counted as 115 eggs were dropped, all in the span of about 5 minutes. They say the odds are that only about 1 in 100 will survive.

WILD WORMS

TAPEWORM

The longest worms on Earth are the bootlace ribbon worm. They normally grow up to 15 feet. However, they can grow to be more than 100 feet long! Which makes them not only the longest worm, but the world's longest animal!

Tapeworms are **parasites**, meaning they prey on a host animal. These worms live in the intestines of mammals and fish. Even humans can find themselves the host of a tapeworm, if they accidentally eat the worm's larva.

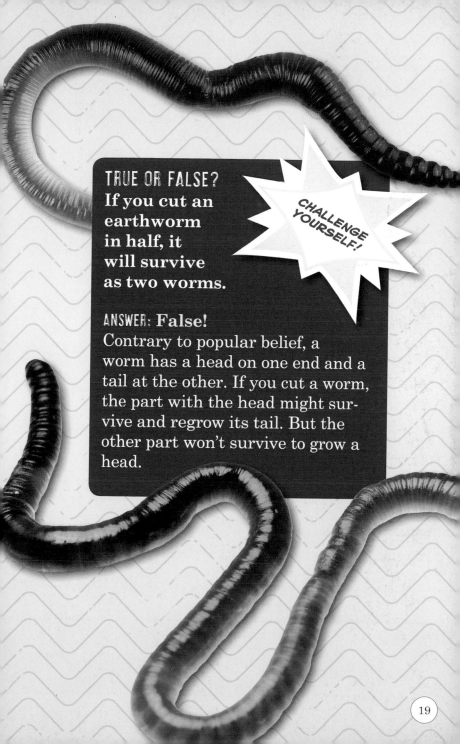

TRUE OR FALSE?
If you cut an
earthworm
in half, it
will survive
as two worms.

CHALLENGE
YOURSELF!

ANSWER: False!
Contrary to popular belief, a
worm has a head on one end and a
tail at the other. If you cut a worm,
the part with the head might survive and regrow its tail. But the
other part won't survive to grow a
head.

Even though they swallow their food whole without chewing it, Atlantic bottlenose dolphins are born with approximately 80 to 100 cone-shaped teeth! And unlike those of sharks, theirs don't grow back!

WORLD'S UGLIEST FISH

STONEFISH

So ugly it hides in plain sight, the camouflaged stonefish is also one of the world's most venomous fish. It is dangerous, even fatal to humans—so much so that there are warnings posted to alert potential victims: "WARNING: The needle-sharp spines of stonefish will easily penetrate bare feet causing severe pain."

I read about a man who survived getting spiked on the finger by a stonefish in Australia. He described the wound as the tiniest of nicks, and yet the fish's venom wreaked havoc on his body. The pain was instant and so intense the man said he actually begged a doctor to amputate his arm! But the doctor talked him out of it.

As the hours passed, the crushing pain traveled up the man's arm to his elbow, then to his shoulder. Soon he couldn't stand up because of the pain in both of his kidneys. Eventually, the intense pain went away, and he slowly got feeling back in his hand. He said he was happy the doctor hadn't amputated, but he still gets kidney pains all these years later!

NIGHT WATCH

Most owls are **nocturnal**, meaning they are awake during the night. But not all! The pygmy owl, for example, is **crepuscular**, meaning it hunts at dawn and dusk. Others, such as the burrowing owl and the short-eared owl, are active during the day, like humans and other animals.

OWL

FALCON

EAGLE

BIRDS OF PREY—including eagles, falcons, owls, osprey, and hawks—all have extremely sharp vision. They use their gifted sight to track their prey at great distances.

CRAZY BUT TRUE

Birds of prey's eyesight can be 10 times better than a human's. A golden eagle, for example, can spot a rabbit from a distance of 2 miles away!

TRUE OR FALSE?
Owls can turn their heads all the way around (360°)!

CHALLENGE YOURSELF!

ANSWER: False!
An owl can turn its head around dramatically, but only about 270°. It actually has to! Unlike humans and other animals, owls have fixed eye sockets and therefore have to turn their heads if they want to look at things directly.

HAWK

baby PENGUINS

BABY PENGUINS

Penguin chicks require attentive parents for survival. Parents feed only their own offspring, identifying their chick by its distinctive call and then regurgitating food into its mouth.

OLDER CHICKS

Chicks hatch with white, gray, black, or brown down feathers, depending on their species. Their down isn't waterproof, and so chicks must stay out of the icy water until their protective feathers grow in. It can take anywhere from 7 weeks to 13 months for juvenile chicks to swim and hunt for their own food.

ROCKHOPPER PENGUINS

To keep their eggs safe from predatory leopard seals, rockhopper penguins nest high up in steep rocky slopes, about 500 feet above sea level.

WHALE SHARK

Though most species of sharks give birth to live young, there are also many species that lay eggs. In fact, an egg of a whale shark (the largest shark in the world, and therefore also the largest fish) was found in the Gulf of Mexico in 1953. It measured 14 inches in diameter—almost 3 times the size of an ostrich egg, the largest egg on land!

TRUE OR FALSE?
**Sharks have teeth
in their mouth
AND on their skin.**

ANSWER: **True!**
While most fish are covered in scales,
sharks have skin covered with tiny plate-
like teeth called **denticles**. They're sharp
enough to give you "shark burn" (similar to
carpet burn) if you rub them the wrong way!

PEREGRINE FALCON
The diving peregrine falcon is the fastest bird, reaching speeds of 200 miles per hour!

OSTRICH
Ostriches can run faster than any other bird—they're able to reach speeds up to 45 miles per hour. They can also run great distances, keeping their speed for 20-mile stretches.

ALBATROSS
Wandering albatrosses boast the greatest wingspan at almost 12 feet!

ONAGADORI
Onagadori, a kind of red jungle fowl, have the longest feathers: 34 ¾ feet.

BIG & fast BIRDS

RÜPPELL'S GRIFFON

Rüppell's griffon vultures are the highest-flying birds, believed to reach an altitude of 7 miles above sea level. (That's almost 8,000 feet higher than Mount Everest, the world's tallest mountain!)

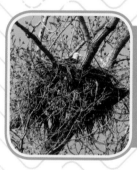

BALD EAGLE NEST

The largest tree nest was built by a bald eagle in Florida. It was 20 feet deep and weighed about 3 tons!

CRAZY BUT TRUE

Harpy eagle parents are similar to human parents in one funny way—they will kick their chicks out of the nest if they refuse to leave home once they're grown!

Photo © Jeff Probst

PORCUPINE HAIR!

PORCUPINE

Porcupine quills aren't poisonous. In fact, they are nothing more than extreme hairs! But that doesn't mean they aren't dangerous. Porcupine quills have one-way barbs that make it difficult for animals to remove them. If left untreated, animals can die from infections caused by quill wounds.

CHALLENGE YOURSELF!

TRUE OR FALSE?
Porcupines are born with their quills.

ANSWER: **True!**
(Though they're soft at the time.)

TRUE OR FALSE?
Quills help porcupines swim.

ANSWER: **True!**
(They help them float!)

WATER-DWELLING REPTILES

TURTLES IN THE SUN

All fish, reptiles, and amphibians are **cold-blooded**. This doesn't mean that their blood is cold, only that their bodies take on the temperature of their surroundings. Many reptiles, for example, will bask in the sun to warm themselves. Being cold-blooded also means that they never run a fever!

A turtle's shell is part of its skeleton. A turtle can't be removed from its shell any easier than a human could be parted with his or her skeleton.

CRAZY BUT TRUE

Alligator snapping turtles have tongues that look like worms, so they can trick fish into swimming directly into their mouths! Talk about clever!

JAPANESE SPIDER CRAB

The world's largest known arthropod, Japanese spider crabs have legs that can grow to be 13 feet long, more than twice the height of the average adult human. They also eat whale carcasses! It takes hundreds of them many years to finish the job, but they do it.

HALLOWEEN CRAB

Colorful Halloween crabs also go by other colorful names, such as moon crabs and Harlequin land crabs. They live in coastal rain forests and eat leaves and small plants.

BOXER CRAB

Also known as "pom-pom crabs," boxer crabs are known to pick up and carry stinging sea anemones for protection. In exchange, the unharmed anemones are able to travel much farther than they could on their own.

PORCELAIN CRAB

Not a "true crab" at all, porcelain crabs are actually a type of lobster! They get their name for being incredibly frag-ile, often losing their limbs when escaping predators. Lucky for them, their limbs grow back!

COCONUT CRAB

The largest land-living arthropod in the world, coconut crabs are giant hermit crabs that take 100 years or more to grow to full size. Usually specimens are about 3 feet long, at which point they have outgrown the need for a protective shell.

There are over 40,000 known spider species in the world, 850 of which are

tarantulas!

CRAZY BUT TRUE

Tarantulas lose their hair when they're frightened!

WANDERING SPIDER OF BRAZIL

Though perhaps less famous than the black widow or the brown recluse, wandering spiders of Brazil are the most poisonous spiders in the world and kill more people than any other.

READ MY LIPS!

Photo © Jeff Probst

NAPOLEON FISH

Living in lagoon reefs and outer reef slopes of the Pacific Ocean, the Indian Ocean, and the Red Sea, Napoleon wrasses are large, almost comical fish. They're also strikingly beautiful up close.

These fish have padded lips, which allow them to eat dangerous, even toxic animals that most other fish leave alone, such as sea urchins, crown-of-thorns starfish, boxfish, and sea hares.

Unfortunately, despite being endangered, Napoleons are considered a prize catch to some fisherman. They are thought to be a delicacy in parts of the world and can be sold for $300 to $400 at restaurants in countries where they aren't protected.

Penguin Parents

PENGUIN NEST

A nest of eggs is called a **clutch**. Penguins usually lay 2 eggs, doubling their chances that at least 1 of their baby chicks will hatch and survive.

A penguin nesting site is called a **rookery**. Penguins usually return to nest in the same rookery from which they themselves hatched, sometimes leading to millions of birds gathering at once.

INCUBATION

Most penguin parents take turns **incubating** their eggs, keeping them warm and safe in their nests. Species that don't build nests incubate single eggs by balancing them on the tops of their feet under a loose fold of warm skin.

EMPEROR PENGUINS

Emperor penguins don't take turns incubating their eggs. A few hours after an egg is laid, the males take over. They incubate the egg for 2 months, not eating until it's ready to hatch. The males lose up to 45% of their body fat during this time.

BLACK-TAILED PRAIRIE DOGS

Black-tailed prairie dogs live in groups called towns, and their world really does resemble a town. Imagine hundreds of animals living and working together on a shared network of tunnels. So their homes are underground, and they literally have specialized "rooms" for sleeping, raising young, and going to the bathroom!

HOME ON THE RANGE

Prairie dogs live in the open plains of North America. Though they are squirrel-like rodents and not canines, prairie dogs bark at danger, wag their short tails, and give birth to litters of "puppies."

Check this out: the largest recorded prairie dog town was in Texas, and it covered 25,000 square miles and housed upward of 400 million prairie dogs. Go impress your buddies with that fact!

BIG Ears, BIG Nose, BIG Everything!

CRAZY BUT TRUE

As heavy as elephants are, they walk on their toes! Elephants' heel bones are actually a good distance off the ground, supported by a cushioned pad. These strange feet allow them to make incredibly long walks. Some can also "run" 24 miles an hour, twice as fast as a human!

Elephants are the largest of all land animals! And African elephants are the largest of all elephants. The biggest elephant on record was more than 13 feet tall and weighed more than 24,000 pounds! That's about as much as a crowd of 150 average-size humans.

Elephants also have the largest noses of any animal on Earth. There are 40,000 muscles and tendons in an elephant's trunk, making it both strong and flexible. Their trunks also have one or two "fingers" that help them grab. Elephants are able to use their trunks to delicately pluck a single blade of grass, or even lift a heavy log! They use them to smell, drink, and bathe.

Weighing about 11 pounds, elephant brains are the largest of any land animal. And they have the largest heads, for that matter. And the largest ears, of course!

SHARK SUPERPOWERS!

Sharks have no bones! Their skeletons are made of light and bendable **cartilage.**

Two-thirds of a shark's brain is devoted to smell. Sharks are able to detect a single drop of blood in an Olympic-size swimming pool and can even tell from which direction a scent is coming!

Sharks have electroreception. All living things give off small electrical signals when they breathe or move. While these signals are too weak for people to pick up on, some sharks are able to sense the electricity of other animals in their surroundings. In fact, some baby shark pups are known to "freeze" when they sense the electric signal of predators approaching.

Sharks have extraordinary hearing. Some are able to hear prey from 3,000 feet away! But unlike dolphins or bats with **echolocation** hearing, sharks listen silently.

CRAZY BUT TRUE

People are 50 times more likely to be killed by bee stings than by shark attacks!

CATERPILLARS

As soon as caterpillars hatch, they eat their eggshell! Then they consume whatever plant they're standing on before roaming in search of even more food. Over the course of several weeks caterpillars will devour 27,000 times their body weight, eventually increasing their size by a 1,000 times.

Caterpillars eat so much because their most important job is to store up enough energy to complete their metamorphosis, ultimately turning into a moth or butterfly.

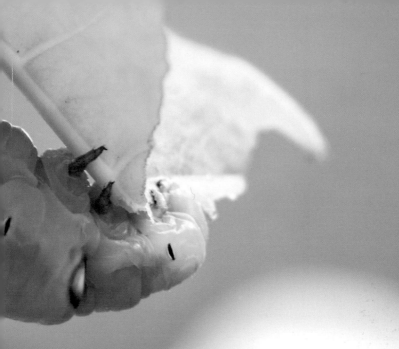

CRAZY BUT TRUE

Some carnivorous caterpillars eat more than plants! The *Liphyra brassolis* butterfly, for example, lays its eggs in an anthill so its caterpillar babies can feast on the ants and their larva. Others eat soft-bodied insects and spiders. Recently, scientists discovered a Hawaiian caterpillar that catches snails in silk webs and then eats everything but the snail shell!

Caterpillars are **insects**, even though they don't have 6 legs. They're technically the larval stage of butterflies and moths.

BARRACUDA

One of the ocean's top **predators**, barracudas are capable of causing serious injury. They have razor-sharp, fang-like teeth and can swim up to 27 miles per hour. As is the case with sharks, barracuda attacks on humans are almost always by mistake. And yet attacks do occur, including one case in which a barracuda jumped out of the water to attack a kayaker!

PIRANHA

Dubbed the "most ferocious fish in the world" by American president Theodore Roosevelt after he witnessed a cow being eaten alive in the Amazon rain forest, piranhas are famous for both their appetites and for ganging up on prey much larger than themselves. Piranhas hunt in large schools (sometimes of a thousand or more), and have extremely sharp teeth capable of biting through a silver hook!

Colorful Bugs

All insects use color for one reason: to survive. Some insects blend in with their surroundings. Others have bright markings to warn potential **predators** that they're poisonous. Others use color to make predators think they're poisonous, copying other bugs.

INSECTS

All insects have exactly 6 legs! Most also have 4 wings and 2 **antennae** on their heads. A great many animals that are commonly believed to be insects aren't actually, including millipedes, spiders, scorpions, and mites.

There are more species of insects than any other group of animals.

CHALLENGE YOURSELF!

ANSWER: **True!**
There are more than a 1,000,000 species of insects. For comparison, there are only about 5,000 species of mammals, 10,000 species of birds, and 32,000 species of fish. There are 20,000 species of butterflies alone!

Creeped out by these creepy crawlers? You're not alone! But insects do a lot of important jobs. They pollinate flowers, loosen the soil, and clean up dead plants and animals by eating their remains. Without insects, there would be few flowers, the soil would be too compact for roots to grow, and dead plants and animals would rot very, very slowly. I'd rather be creeped out by bugs than by dead animal bodies everywhere! How about you?

SNAKEHEAD FISH

Though they're relativly small (3 feet long, at most), snakehead fish are top-level predators known to attack anything in sight while they are breeding. But that's not the scariest thing about them. Invasive species are a serious problem because they disrupt local ecosystems, displacing native populations. Originally from Asia, snakeheads have established themselves in every corner of the United States, wreaking havoc in Maryland, California, and Florida. Individual fish have been caught in Maine, Massachusetts, Rhode Island, Hawaii, and elsewhere.

CRAZY BUT TRUE

Snakeheads can breathe air and survive out of water for up to 4 days! They're so hearty, in fact, that, according to Florida fisheries scientist Kelly Gestring, once a snakehead population establishes itself, "neither man nor nature can get rid of them."

LIVING FOSSILS

HORSESHOE CRAB
Horseshoe crabs are often called living fossils because their bodies have changed so little in the 450 million years they have inhabited the Earth. Despite their name, horseshoe crabs have more in common with spiders and other arachnids than with true crabs!

OSTRICH

The ostrich is the largest flightless bird (both the heaviest and the tallest). It is also the largest living bird, period.

Ostriches have the largest eyes of any land animal and they lay the largest eggs. The largest egg on record was laid by an ostrich in Borlänge, Sweden, in 2008. It weighed 5 pounds, 11.36 ounces!

Which is the only bird to hunt using its sense of smell?

A ostrich

C emu

B penguin

D kiwi

ANSWER: **D!**
The only birds to have external nostrils at the tip of their long beaks, kiwis sniff out seeds, grubs, worms, and other small invertebrates. They are believed to have the keenest sense of smell of nearly all birds, second only to the condor.

Which of the following have virtually nonexistent tail feathers?

A kiwi

C rhea

E all of the above

B emu

D cassowary

ANSWER: **E!**
These flightless birds have virtually no tail feathers. Do you think that's why they can't fly?

BEE HUMMINGBIRD

True!

CHALLENGE YOURSELF!

CHALLENGE YOURSELF!

True!

4,500

Hummingbirds fly like helicopters, rotating each wing in a circle. Unlike most birds, they can move in all sorts of directions and hover in midair, and they are the ONLY bird that can fly backward!

63

WHAT A BULLY!

BULL SHARK

The most likely shark to attack humans, bull sharks have the strongest bite force of any living fish species. Plus, they're able to live in freshwater.

GOLIATH BIRD-EATING SPIDER

Found in swampy areas of South American rain forests, goliath bird-eaters are **nocturnal** and have the second largest leg span of any spider in the world. Though officially slightly smaller than the giant huntsman, goliath spiders are heavier. They also have 1-inch-long fangs! And yes, they can and do eat birds.

GIANT SPIDERS

GIANT HUNTSMAN SPIDER

Considered the largest spider in the world, giant huntsman spiders have a 12-inch leg span! Cave dwellers by nature, these spiders were first discovered in Southeast Asia in 2001. They have since been found elsewhere, including in 2013 in the United Kingdom, when one of the giant spiders was found in a shipment arriving from Taiwan.

Vultures eat dead and rotting **carcasses**. A vulture's stomach is more acidic than those of other animals. They're able to eat meat that would make other animals sick.

BLACK VULTURE

Vultures are social birds. They often feed, fly, or roost in large flocks. They're so social, in fact, that a group of vultures goes by many names: a wake, a committee, a venue, a volt, or a kettle, all depending on what the group is doing.

Photo © Jeff Probst

TRUE OR FALSE?
Vultures circling is a sign that something is dead or dying.

ANSWER: **False!** When vultures circle, they're actually soaring up on warm and rising pockets of air. After they have gained some altitude, they'll continue sweeping their territory. Vultures don't hesitate to descend on a potential meal! They can tell very quickly if something is dead, even at great distances.

HOW to Make a Pearl!

Oysters, clams, and mussels are all capable of producing pearls, but oyster pearls are the most common. Pearls form when a foreign substance—such as a grain of sand—makes its way into a closed oyster by mistake. It's similar to when a human gets a splinter! The oyster responds by coating the sand with **nacre**, the same thing that coats the inside of the shell as it grows. As the oyster continues to grow, the sand gets covered by more and more layers of nacre, very slowly growing in size.

MUSSELS

CLAMS

OYSTER WITH
PEARL

REAL-LIFE DRAGONS!

KOMODO DRAGON

The largest of all lizards, komodo dragons can be more than 10 feet long and weigh more than 350 pounds! They are venomous lizards, yet their venom isn't the worst part of their bite. Komodo dragon mouths are full of dangerous bacteria. If an animal survives an attack from one of these giant lizards, it likely won't survive the blood poisoning that follows. Komodo dragons will stalk their dying prey for a week or more before feasting. And when they finally get to have their meal, they eat almost everything—even the bones!

SQUIRREL

RODENTS

More than 2,000 species of rodents get their name from the Latin word *rodere*, which means "to gnaw."

Because their **incisors** continue to grow for as long as they live, many rodents will chew through nearly anything—even concrete—to keep their teeth short and sharp.

BEAVER

CRAZY BUT TRUE

Mice can fit through a hole no wider than a pencil!

The world's largest rodent is the capybara, also known as a water hog. It can grow to 4 feet long and weigh 150 pounds. In other words, it's a rat the size of a large dog! Imagine that hiding under your fridge!

NIGHTMARE SHARK

Sharks predate the dinosaurs! Scientists have discovered fossils of sharks that lived 300 million years ago.

SHARK TEETH

SHARK JAW

Great white sharks are the largest **carnivorous** fish living today, but there was a time when sharks were three times bigger! Believe that! In fact, the monstrous *Carcharodon megalodon* had jaws big enough to swallow a small car!

BUBBLE BOMBER!

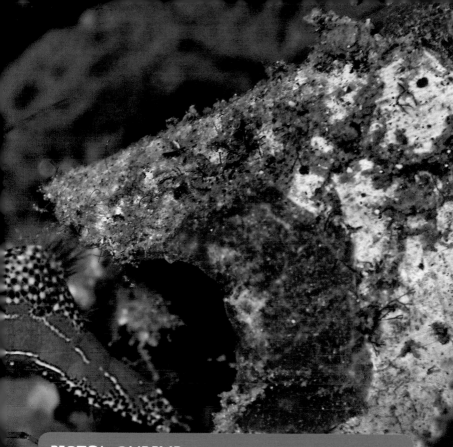

PISTOL SHRIMP

Pistol shrimp only grow to be 1 or 2 inches long. And yet these small crustaceans compete with sperm whales and beluga whales for the title of loudest animal in the sea! By snapping its specialized claw, a pistol shrimp releases an incredibly loud underwater bubble that can reach speeds of 60 miles per hour, able to kill small fish on impact. The bubbles also create momentary heat approaching the temperature of the sun and collective noise capable of disturbing human sonar systems!

MAN'S BEST FRIEND

WOLVES

Wolves are the ancestors of domesticated dogs. Early in human history, people began using wild dogs to help them hunt and to protect their homes. Over many thousands of years, dogs became increasingly trusting of humans, and vice versa. Today, out of all of the animals in the animal world, dogs are considered "man's best friend."

DOGS

Though the domesticated dog evolved over countless **millennia**, the 350 to 400 breeds of dogs recognized today have been around for only a couple hundred years. Dog breeders selectively mix the **genes** of different dogs to bring out desired characteristics.

CRAZY BUT TRUE

Scientists have found that all dog breeds still carry wolf-like traits in their genetic profile. Many breeds were even revealed to possess a majority of wolf-like genes, suggesting that they are among the oldest domesticated breeds! These include Shiba Inus, chow chows, Akitas, Alaskan malamutes, basenjis, Chinese shar-peis, Siberian huskies, and Afghan hounds.

DO LOBSTERS HAVE FEELINGS?

LOBSTER

For hundreds of years scientists and philosophers have argued about the nature of suffering and whether invertebrate animals— such as crustaceans and insects— are capable of experiencing physical pain the way humans and other animals do. To this day, scientists aren't completely sure!

Some believe that the lack of nerves and a spine means that lobsters, crabs, and other crustaceans don't have feelings the way humans do. Others point to evidence that lobsters and crabs show signs of stress and even desperation beyond that of predictable reflex.

QUESTION
**Why do lobsters turn
red when cooked?**

ANSWER: In the wild, lobsters usually appear a muddy brownish green.
A rare few look blue or orange. But they
all turn red when cooked. That's because
their bodies contain **pigments**, or colors, to
help them blend into their surroundings. One
of the pigments, called astaxanthin, is red.
While most of their colors burn away when
heated, astaxanthin doesn't. With only red
pigment remaining, that's the color we see!

Rhino You Are, but What Am I?

Did you know the name *rhinoceros* is made of two Greek words meaning

"nose" & *"horn"*?

A type of giant rhinoceros called an Indricotherium is thought to be the largest land mammal that ever lived! It stood 28 feet tall!

White rhinos, the largest species of rhino, can weigh up to 2,000 pounds, and they are the second largest animal on land.

Rhinos are also the only animals with a horn on their noses instead of on the tops of their heads!

Some historians believe that elephants and rhinos were the real-life inspiration for stories about mythical animals, such as unicorns and *cyclopes!*

CRAZY BUT TRUE

Travelers returning from Africa to Europe told stories about rhinos they saw. But without photographs, all they could do was describe the animals or draw pictures. Early sketches of rhinos looked like a horse with a big horn! Sounds like a unicorn, right?

ELEPHANT SKULL

Ever see an elephant skull? The eyeholes are all the way at the sides, while the nose hole for the trunk is larger and right in the center. Somebody who saw the skull without seeing a living elephant might have thought it belonged to a one-eyed giant.

CURIOUS CANINES

Wolves, foxes, jackals, and coyotes—as well as domesticated dogs—are all canines, meaning they are part of the family Canidae.

JACKAL

WOLF

COYOTE

FOX

CRAZY BUT TRUE

Wolves have unique howls! Just like human fingerprints, scientists can tell wolves apart by studying their voices. That's also how a wolf pack knows which calls are coming from their pack leader.

Unlikely Arthropods

WHAT A PILL!
Though they're called bugs, pill bugs are actually crustaceans. They have too many legs to be an insect. They also have too many antennae!

CRAZY BUT TRUE

Pill bugs breathe through gills! They need moist air to breathe and can survive underwater. They also don't pee! While most animals convert ammonia-rich waste into urine, pill bugs don't have a problem with ammonia. Instead of peeing, their waste passes out through their **exoskeleton**.

Centipedes and millipedes aren't insects, either. Centipede means "hundred-legged" and millipede means "thousand-legged." While they don't literally have that many legs, they have far more than 6. Though they aren't crustaceans, like pill bugs, they are closer relatives with lobsters and crabs than they are with flies or even beetles.

MILLIPEDE   CENTIPEDE

LION'S MANE JELLYFISH

Lion's mane jellyfish, or hair jellyfish, are the largest known type of jellyfish. They have stinging tentacles that reach 100 feet in length.

IRUKANDJI JELLYFISH

The small but horrifying Irukandji jellyfish are a type of box jellyfish able to fire their venomous stingers into their victim, causing searing pain, cramps, vomiting, and other symptoms.

Around the world, humans are stung by jellyfish an estimated

150 million

times every year.

SEA WASP JELLYFISH

Commonly known as sea wasp jellyfish, the *Chironex fleckeri*—a kind of box jellyfish—are considered "the most lethal jellyfish in the world." They are also among the smartest, complete with a brain and sophisticated eyes.

Photo © Jeff Probst

Not all jellyfish sting people! In Palau there is a place called Jellyfish Lake—which is about 12,000 years old. It's filled with golden jellyfish, which, over the years, have lost their necessity to sting. So even though they still have stinging cells called **cnidocytes**, they are not powerful enough to cause pain to the average person. It was one of the coolest experiences of my life to swim with thousands of jellyfish, knowing I couldn't get stung!

SLOWLY BUT SURELY!

Giant tortoises can live 150 years or more! According to Guinness World Records, the oldest tortoise of all time was Tui Malila, who died in Tonga in 1965 at the age of 189.

The oldest known tortoise alive today is named Jonathan. Born February 7, 1832, he lives on the island of Saint Helena, in the south Atlantic Ocean.

GECKO

I SEE YOU...

Almost all species of geckos lack eyelids. They instead have a clear membrane over their eyes, which they have to lick clean since they are not equipped to blink.

Green iguanas have a third eye. It's a small, transparent scale on the top of their heads that sees just enough to detect movement from above.

CHALLENGE YOURSELF!

What reptile can move its eyes in two different directions at once?

A box turtle   **C** chameleon

B basilisk lizard   **D** crocodile

ANSWER: **C!**

Also famous for its ability to change colors to match its surroundings, the chameleon is the only lizard that can see in two directions at once!

What lizard can squirt blood out of its eyes?

A komodo dragon   **C** dwarf gecko

B sea turtle   **D** horned lizard

ANSWER: **D!**

At least 4 species of horned lizards are able to squirt an aimed stream of foul-tasting blood out of the corners of their eyes; the stream of blood can reach up to 5 feet.

SPIDER WASPS

TARANTULA HAWK WASP

With hooked grappling claws, a metallic blue body, and fiery red wings, the tarantula hawk wasp—named for the spiders it hunts—is a spectacle to be seen. It also has a paralyzing sting, considered the second most painful insect sting in the world!

The tarantula hawk itself feeds on fruit nectar. It's when the wasp reproduces that it becomes particularly violent. The female stings and paralyzes a tarantula much larger than herself, and then drags it back to her nest still alive. She then lays her eggs on the spider's abdomen before sealing the nest shut. When the eggs hatch, the wasp larvae burrow into the spider, feeding on it for several weeks, trying not to kill it. Eventually, the wasps burrow out of the spider and up out of the ground.

Tarantula hawks are the largest wasps in the United States! They have been designated the official state insect of New Mexico, and have been spotted as far north as Goldendale, Washington.

POISONOUS AMPHIBIANS

POISON DART FROG

Identifiable from their brightly colored skin, poison dart frogs got their name after people in the South American rain forest started to use their toxins on darts and other weapons.

SPANISH RIBBED NEWT

The only amphibian actually capable of injecting venom, the Spanish ribbed newt not only secretes poison onto its skin, but it has sharp ribs that it will force through its own skin if provoked. The poison-laced ribs act as a highly effective stinging mechanism until the newt's skin heals.

CANE TOAD

Potentially lethal to humans and other animals, the cane toad secretes a milky poison onto its skin when threatened. One side effect of cane toad poisoning involves temporary hallucinations. Though dangerous, some people actually milk cane toads for their toxins in order to use them as recreational drugs.

CORAL
Corals, at the center of coral reefs, are living invertebrates. These "rain forests of the sea" are some of the most complex **ecosystems** on Earth.

COLORFUL CORAL!

BY LEAPS AND BOUNDS

The world's largest frog, the goliath frog, can leap 9 feet, about 9 times the length of its body.

GOLIATH FROG

The world's smallest frog, the gold frog, can jump only about 12 inches—but that's more than 20 times its body length.

GOLDEN FROG

Wallace's flying frog has them both beat—it's able to jump and "glide" like a flying squirrel. Doing this, it can make leaps of around 50 feet! That's 100 times the length of its body!

FLYING FROG

FLYING MAMMALS

Bats are the only mammals that can truly fly! There are nearly 1,000 species of bats, and they can be found in more climates and habitats than nearly any other animal.

BLIND AS A BAT

It is true that bats can't see very well. But they don't need to! Bats hunt at night. They use other senses to find their food. Some hunt insects with **echolocation**, listening carefully for echoes of their own calls, which bounce off bugs in the air.

Some bats eat fish, others eat fruit, and a few even drink blood! But most bats eat insects at night, thus playing a crucial role for humans by eating mosquitoes and some of the insects that destroy our crops.

Most bats are small enough to fit in your hand! The largest bat is the giant golden-crowned flying fox. It can grow to be as big as 5 ½ feet! But don't worry, it eats fruit, not blood. And unfortunately, it's endangered.

GIANT
GOLDEN-CROWNED
FLYING FOX

HIP-HIPPO-HOORAY!

The common hippopotamus is the third-largest animal on land. The name is Greek for "river horse," but hippos are more closely related to pigs than to horses. They have similar eyes, ears, and hooves. They also love the mud!

Hippos are **nocturnal**. Hippos graze on grass at night, and they hide in water during the day (they're very good at this).

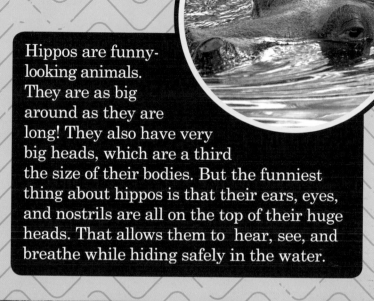

Hippos are funny-looking animals. They are as big around as they are long! They also have very big heads, which are a third the size of their bodies. But the funniest thing about hippos is that their ears, eyes, and nostrils are all on the top of their huge heads. That allows them to hear, see, and breathe while hiding safely in the water.

Girls Don't Sing!

More than half of all birds (including song-birds) are **passerines**, meaning they belong to the order Passeriformes. Their most distinctive features are their toes! Three point forward and one points backward—which makes perching easier. More than 5,000 species fit into that order, and the males usually have colorful feathers, beaks, and legs to show off how healthy they are, while the female hens are less showy.

SONGBIRD

Have you ever heard a songbird in the spring? It was a male.

Surprised? Boy birds sing to attract mates, and then they sing again to let everybody know they had chicks! The males also teach their offspring their song. And if that isn't enough, it's also the job of the males to sing the melody. Females can chirp, but only one note.

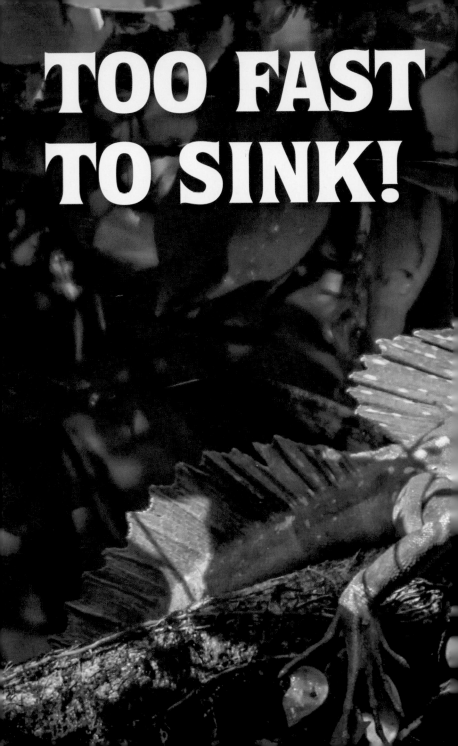

TOO FAST
TO SINK!

BASILISK LIZARD
Though they live mostly on land, basilisk lizards are able to walk—or rather, run—on water! When they sense danger, they dash on their hind legs quickly enough that their huge splayed feet don't allow them to sink, earning their nickname, the Jesus lizard. Measuring 4 inches from head to tail, basilisk lizards are the largest animal to do this.

HAPPY 1,000TH BIRTHDAY!

Sponges do not have heads, arms, or internal organs, and yet they are considered animals. This is because, unlike plants that use **photosynthesis** to make their own food, sponges filter food to obtain nutrients from the water.

BARREL SPONGE

The largest sponges in the world are barrel sponges, which grow to be 50 feet across. They're called the "redwoods of the deep" because some of them are an estimated 2,400 years old!

CRAZY BUT TRUE

Some sponges sneeze! Demosponges, the largest group of sponges, remove unwanted materials from their bodies much like people do. Sensing inedible particles in the water, they respond by contracting and forcing water out, along with whatever was irritating them.

Some species of sponges in the ocean near Antarctica are thought to be 10,000 years old! Imagine if you had a sponge that old in your sink. Whoa!

SNAKE FACTS

After they hatch on land, snakes survive on their own (without help from their parents)!

Snakes can't see color! Though some snakes can see temperatures in infrared!

PIT VIPER

Snake scales are made of keratin (the same material that makes up human fingernails).

Snakes hear using their skin! And can smell using their tongue!

Most snakes are nonvenomous (and less than 2% are considered dangerous to humans).

ROUGH GREEN SNAKE

Snakes breathe by flexing their rib cage. Some even have 3 lungs!

MICRURUS NIGROCINCTUS

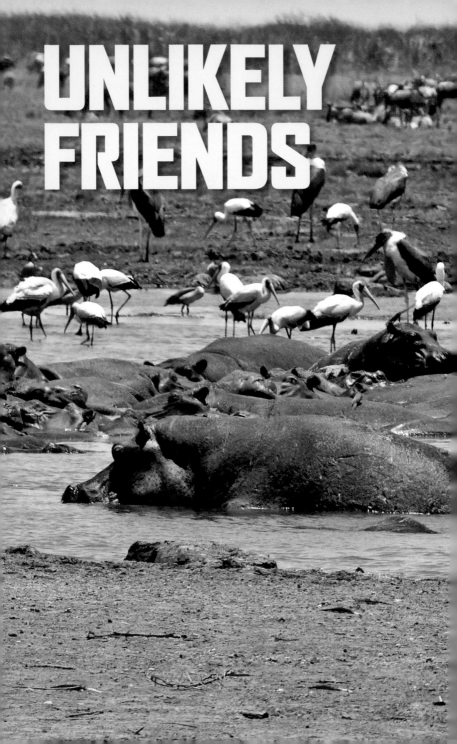

UNLIKELY FRIENDS

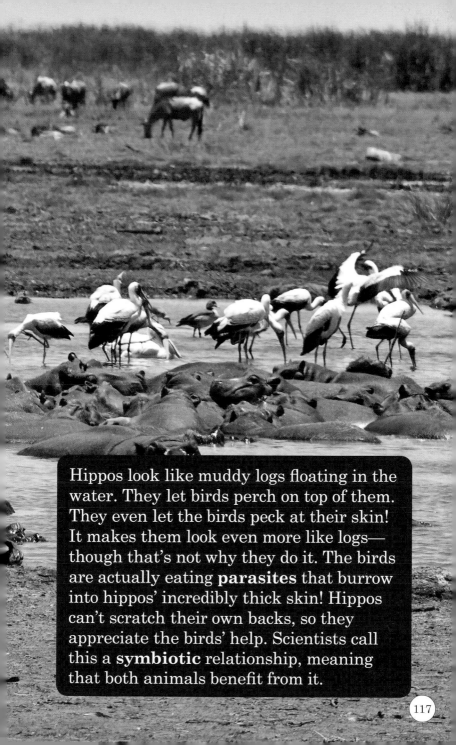

Hippos look like muddy logs floating in the water. They let birds perch on top of them. They even let the birds peck at their skin! It makes them look even more like logs— though that's not why they do it. The birds are actually eating **parasites** that burrow into hippos' incredibly thick skin! Hippos can't scratch their own backs, so they appreciate the birds' help. Scientists call this a **symbiotic** relationship, meaning that both animals benefit from it.

GREAT APES

GORILLA

The largest primates in the world, gorillas live in the forests of Africa. Silverback gorillas can weigh 390 pounds or more, and they are believed to be 15 times stronger than humans.

ORANGUTAN

The most **solitary** of the great apes, orangutans spend most of their time in trees. Average adults have a reach of 8 feet, roughly twice their own height. No wonder they're so good at swinging from branch to branch, high up in the rain forest canopy!

CHIMPANZEE

Some chimpanzees have learned to "talk" using American Sign Language (ASL) and computer programs. The first chimp to learn ASL, named Washoe, learned 350 words. When she first saw a swan, she impressed researchers by identifying it as a "water bird"!

BONOBO

Belonging to the same family as chimpanzees, bonobos are found in only one part of the world: the Congo Basin in Central Africa. Unlike chimpanzees, bonobos are female dominant, less aggressive, and do not hunt in groups or use tools. In terms of problem solving, bonobos are thought to be more like humans than any other animals on Earth!

small apes

CHALLENGE
YOURSELF!

Which of the following is a characteristic of gibbons that is DIFFERENT from great apes?

A Adult males and females are roughly the same size.

B Gibbon couples often mate for life.

C They don't make nests.

D All of the above.

ANSWER: **D!**

GIBBONS

Though often confused with monkeys, there are more than a dozen species of gibbons, which are also considered apes. Like larger apes, these primates have no tails.

MONKEY OR APE?

The easiest way to tell the difference between apes and monkeys is to look for a tail! Only monkeys have tails. Apes do not.

Apes are also larger than monkeys. They have an upright posture and broader chests. Apes have shoulders that allow them to swing from branch to branch, while monkeys run along the tops of branches the way a cat or dog might.

SPIDER MONKEY

121

Meat Eaters

There are more than 250 species of **carnivores**. Because they have adapted to catch and eat other animals, some of the world's most efficient **predators** are meat eaters, including lions, tigers, some bears, and wolves.

Obligate carnivores, or "true" carnivores, depend on animal flesh and organs for their survival. Their stomachs are unable to digest plants and other non-meat foods. Cats, including house cats, are among the world's only true carnivores. Some animals are carnivorous in nature but are able to survive on plants when fresh meat is hard to come by.

FLAMINGO

DOVE

BiRD MiLK

Pigeons, doves, flamingos, and some penguins can excrete a kind of milk produced in their **crop**, the part of their gullet that stores food before it's digested. Bird milk is rich in fats and protein, but unlike mammalian milk, it does not contain calcium or carbohydrates. Just like in mammals, however, the milk is the perfect food for young chicks not yet ready to eat adult food.

Adult flamingos are **filter feeders**, meaning they eat by straining loose food out of water, much like whales eat krill. Flamingos eat with their heads upside down in the water, using their tongues to suck blue-green algae and small shrimp through their bills to be swallowed. Because they use their tongues so actively, flamingos have the longest, fleshiest tongues of any bird.

CHALLENGE YOURSELF!

TRUE OR FALSE?
Birds fart!

ANSWER: **True!**
In fact, the bassian thrush of eastern Australia reportedly uses flatulence to startle worms and insects, causing them to reveal their locations. That's one way to catch your prey!

DEEP DIVERS

NARWHAL WHALE

Identifiable for their massive ivory horns, the narwhal is among the deepest-diving whales. Being mammals and not fish, all whales have to come to the surface to breathe. Yet narwhals are able to dive more than a mile deep, holding their breath for 25 minutes or more.

Aside from their deepest dives, narwhals spend a remarkable amount of time a half mile below the surface. They spend more than 3 hours a day swimming up and down in complete darkness and under intense pressure.

The deepest-diving whale is the Cuvier's beaked whale. Scientists tracked one on a nearly 2-mile dive. The whale was below the surface of the water for roughly 2 hours and 17 minutes. That's some held breath!

NATURAL DECORATORS

Bowerbirds build nests like no other birds. To make up for their relatively plain coloration and lack of song, male bowerbirds construct an elaborate bower, or room, complete with thatched walls and a roof. They even go as far as to decorate their home with prized objects from their surroundings—shiny acorns, snail shells, flowers, stones, and more.

Depending on their habitat, bowerbirds will scavenge for coins, nails, and colorful bits of glass or plastic. Once collected, the birds will spend hours arranging the objects—all in the hope of luring a mate.

Mollusks

include slugs, snails, octopuses, squid, clams, and mussels.

OCTOPUSES

Octopuses have 3 hearts! Their blood is different than the blood of land animals, allowing them to live in cold water and at great depths. Because their blood holds less oxygen, though, octopuses need 3 hearts to keep it all moving through their bodies.

EXTREME MOLLUSKS

SNAILS

Snails can carry up to 10 times their own body weight, even when climbing sideways in a vertical direction. That's like a person carrying a cow up the side of a building!

CRAZY BUT TRUE

Some mollusks can live a very long time. One famous ocean quahog clam (named Ming) lived to be 507 years old!

ALLIGATOR FACTS

ALLIGATOR

Alligators are fast! Even with their short legs, alligators can outrun all but the fastest humans. But don't worry about being chased by one. They most often sprint to escape from danger, preferring to sneak up on their prey.

Alligators are known for their long mouths and sharp teeth, yet they prefer to kill their prey by drowning it. Sometimes, they even perform a "death roll" underwater by spinning their muscular tails.

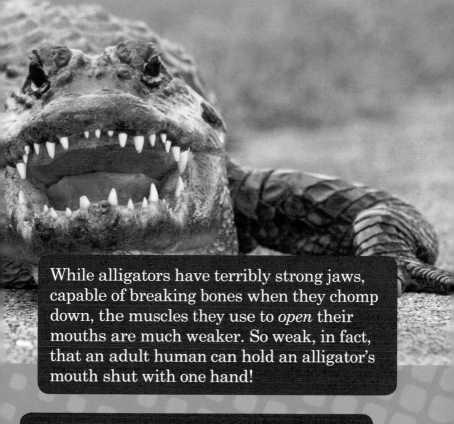

While alligators have terribly strong jaws, capable of breaking bones when they chomp down, the muscles they use to *open* their mouths are much weaker. So weak, in fact, that an adult human can hold an alligator's mouth shut with one hand!

ALLIGATOR EYE
Like crocodiles, alligators have 2 sets of eyelids! One set is clear and helps them see underwater. (Think that's a lot? Camels have 3!)

HONEY BADGER

Despite their small size, honey badgers are considered one of the world's most fearless creatures. Carnivorous in nature, honey badgers will eat insects, frogs, tortoises, rodents, turtles, lizards, snakes, eggs, and birds. They will hunt any time of day or night, if necessary, and have even been known to chase away lion cubs to steal from them.

Aiding in their fearlessness, honey badgers' skin protects them. It is both too thick to be penetrated by stings and bites and loose enough that honey badgers can turn around within their skin to strike any animal trying to hold them in place. Talk about cool! I dare you to try that one! Go ahead, try to turn around in your own skin. You can't do it!

BLUE WHALE

By far, the largest known animal on Earth is the blue whale. Fully grown, they can measure 100 feet from head to tail and weigh as much as 150 tons (300,000 pounds). That's the length of 3 school buses (and the weight of 15 school buses)! Yet despite their size and power, blue whales almost exclusively eat krill, shrimp-like crustaceans roughly the size of a paper clip.

WORLD'S LARGEST ANIMAL

CRAZY BUT TRUE

A blue whale's heart alone is the size of a small car. Its tongue is as heavy as an elephant. Its blowhole can shoot a spray of water 3 stories high! Blue whales are so huge that they have blood vessels big enough for a human to swim through!

There are 264 species of monkeys, all non-ape **primates**.

Howler monkeys live in Latin American rain forests and are among the largest of the New World monkeys. They're also the loudest! Hence the name.

HOWLER MONKEY

We recently shot *Survivor* in Nicaragua, which is in Central America, and howler monkeys are everywhere! So every day when I would drive through the jungle, I would hear them howling away in the trees. One time when my son and daughter were visiting, we got out of the car and walked into the jungle until we found a family of howler monkeys sitting up in a tree. They were checking us out, but they were really quiet. So we started imitating their howl, and whaddaya know, they howled back at us! It was awesome. Even though we had no idea what they were saying, we kinda felt like we were talking with them!

GELADA BABOON

OLD WORLD MONKEY

Monkeys are divided into 2 groups, Old World monkeys (which live in Africa and Asia), and New World monkeys (which live in Central and South America). Aside from where they live, the 2 groups have distinct differences. New World monkeys have grasping tails, for example, while Old World monkeys don't.

NEW WORLD MONKEY

GOLDEN LION TAMARIN

Miles beneath the ocean's surface, too deep for sunlight, fascinating and sometimes terrifying creatures lurk in vast realms of darkness. Deep-ocean animals have found a way to live, and sometimes hunt, where few other animals can.

FANGTOOTH

Fangtooth fish have the largest teeth in the ocean. In fact, their teeth are so large the fish can't fully close their mouths. They're among the deepest-living fish, found swimming 16,400 feet below sea level.

DEEP-SEA ANGLERFISH

Perhaps the best-known deep-sea creature, deep-sea anglerfish have an elongated dorsal spine, with which they dangle a light-producing organ called a **photophore**. Their gaping mouths and pliable bodies allow them to swallow prey attracted to the **bioluminescent** lure, including fish up to twice their size.

COLOSSAL SQUID

Growing to between 39 and 46 feet, colossal squid are the largest known invertebrates in the world. Unlike their relative the giant squid, colossal squid are armed with sharp hooks, which they use to combat sperm whales, sleeper sharks, and other natural predators.

SCAVENGERS
OF THE
SKIES!

BEARDED VULTURE

The bearded vulture is the only bird that deliberately dyes its feathers. He does this by rubbing himself in wet red clay, then letting the clay dry.

But why?

Animal behavior biologist Antoni Margalida believes the vultures dye their feathers to make up for a lack of coloration due to the bird's incredibly limited diet. Bearded vultures specifically eat carcasses of animals that fell from rocks and cliffs, surviving only on bone marrow or whatever else other scavengers leave behind. According to Margalida, the red color is a kind of "status symbol." It's possible that the vultures are attempting to look more nourished than they are.

DUCK WALK

Ducks and other waterfowl are graceful in water, but they sure can seem awkward on land! That's because the best swimmers have legs far back on their bodies. While this adaptation makes their swimming stance more powerful, it makes them off balance, with the majority of their weight in front of them. Ducks have to walk carefully, or else they'll fall forward!

DUCK

CASSOWARY

TURKEY

ROOSTER

Roosters, turkeys, cassowaries, Muscovy ducks, and other birds are remarkable for their **carbuncles**—fleshy growths on their faces and under their necks. A carbuncle dangling under a bird's face is called a wattle. One dangling from a turkey's forehead is called a snood. Though considered ugly by human standards, carbuncles play a large part in how these birds find a mate!

LEECH

Leeches are worms with suckers at each end that live in shallow, slow-moving freshwater. Some have sharp teeth and suck blood. Some attack only fish, while others attack anything—including people! In fact, it used to be common practice for doctors to use leeches to draw patients' blood as part of a medical procedure.

CRAZY BUT TRUE

Leeches are still used in modern medicine! Sometimes they're attached to patients during skin graft procedures, when skin is moved from one part of the body to another. Leeches contain natural blood thinners, which help the wounded area more gently accept the new skin.

When we were shooting *Survivor* in the Amazon, leeches were a major nuisance! It was very common to come back from a day's work and have several of them attached to your legs. It's a really strange, icky feeling. The way we got them off was to slide a fingernail or something like the blade of a pocketknife under the front of them and quickly slide them off onto the ground.

RHINO IN THE MUD

Rhinos have thick skin, but it is still very sensitive. These animals get sunburned easily and are prone to insect bites. For this reason, rhinos spend a lot of time rolling in mud, covering themselves with a protective layer of clay. Good luck finding a "white" or "black" rhino, despite their names. Rhinos usually appear the color of whatever mud they last rolled in!

RHINO HORNS

Unfortunately for rhinos, their horns are part of why these animals are critically endangered. People hunt the animals to steal their horns. Some cultures believe that rhino horns have magical healing powers. Even though scientists have proved that fact untrue, people still pay a lot of money for rhino horns. Made of the same stuff as human fingernails, rhino horns are worth more than gold.

VAMPIRE BATS!

There are only 3 species of vampire bats, and they all live in Central and South America, where they feed off the blood of cows and other sleeping livestock. Chemicals in their saliva numb their bites so that the animals don't wake up.

While the bats have razor-sharp fangs, they don't actually suck blood. Instead, they lick blood up with their tongues through a special gap in their bottom lips!

CRAZY BUT TRUE

Vampire bats can run, and faster than you'd think! While most bats are able to move fast only in the air, vampire bats can run on the ground, using all 4 limbs to push themselves forward at speeds of more than 3 feet per second!

WHAT'S A MONOTREME?

PLATYPUS

The word *monotreme* means "single opening" in Greek. Unlike most mammals, **monotremes** poop, pee, and reproduce using the same part of the body, called the **cloaca**.

Monotremes are also the only mammals that lay and carry eggs instead of giving live birth. Mother monotremes provide milk to their young directly from their skin into their dense fur, to be licked up by their babies.

There are only 5 living species of monotremes: the duck-billed platypus and 4 types of echidna, or spiny anteaters. They are native only to Australia and New Guinea!

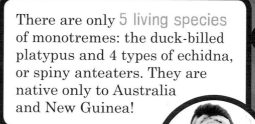

ECHIDNA

LIVING SPIKY BALLS

SPINY ANTEATER

Spiny anteaters, or echidnas, are timid, and they curl into a ball to protect themselves. Covered with spines like a porcupine, spiny anteaters eat ants and termites by lapping them up with a long sticky tongue. They don't have any teeth—the insides of their mouths are covered with spines that grind up bugs for food!

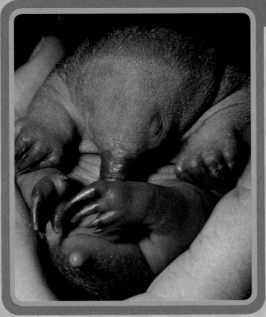

CRAZY BUT TRUE

Echidnas' rear feet point backward! This **adaptation** helps them push away soil as they dig.

PLATYPUS

When European naturalists saw platypuses in 1798, they thought someone was playing a trick on them! Platypuses have a bill like a duck, a tail like a beaver, and webbed feet like an otter. They lay eggs like a lizard, shoot poison out of a spur on their feet, are covered in fur, and can sense electrical signals with their bill.

CHALLENGE YOURSELF!

Which animal is about the size of an average platypus?

 A A mouse   **C** A house cat

 B A guinea pig   **D** A beaver

ANSWER: **C!**

CHALLENGE YOURSELF!

In which of the following countries have fossils of ancient relatives of platypuses been found?

A United States   **C** Greenland

B Argentina   **D** South Africa

ANSWER: **B!**

Platypus babies have teeth,
but the adults do not.

Platypuses? Platypi? Platypodes?
There is no universally
agreed-upon plural for

platypus.

SURVIVAL TIPS!

HOW TO AVOID A SHARK ATTACK:

▼ If you see a shark while swimming, get out of the water. And be sure to warn others about what you saw.

▼ Don't swim in murky water. Sharks don't want to bite people (humans are not their favorite food), but sharks sometimes get confused.

▼ Never swim alone. Sharks are less likely to attack people in groups.

▼ If you have a cut, stay out of the water. Sharks are attracted to blood from very far away.

IF YOU ARE ATTACKED BY A SHARK, HERE'S HOW TO PROTECT YOURSELF:

▼ Don't panic. If a shark bites you, it's most likely by mistake. If you thrash around in the water, it will be more likely to stay interested in you.

▼ Punch it in the face! Sharks have very sensitive noses. A blow to almost any part of the head will tell a shark you're not the defenseless fish he thought you were.

GLOSSARY

ADAPTATION: A feature that assists in an animal's survival. There are both structural and behavioral adaptations.

ANTENNA: A sensitive organ on the head of insects and crustaceans, used for touch, smell, and taste.

BIOLUMINESCENT: Light created and emitted from a living organism.

CARBUNCLE: A fleshy, red growth on the face or head, such as the waddle of a turkey.

CARCASS: The body of a dead animal.

CARNIVORE: An animal that feeds on the flesh of other animals.

CARTILAGE: Translucent, flexible tissue that forms bendable skeletal structures inside animals.

CLOACA: A digestive and reproductive opening present in amphibians, reptiles, birds, some fish, and monotreme mammals (but no others).

CLUTCH: A group of bird, amphibian, or reptile eggs produced at the same time.

CNIDOCYTE: A venomous, exploding cell found only in the phylum Cnidaria (corals, sea anemones, jellyfish, etc.).

COLD-BLOODED: An animal whose body temperature changes with its surroundings.

CREPUSCULAR: Active at dawn and dusk.

CROP: A part of the digestive tract of birds and insects that stores food between the mouth and the stomach.

DENTICLE: Tooth-like projections.

ECHOLOCATION: A way for animals to find food or avoid obstacles by giving off a series of sounds, then listening for the echoes bouncing off objects and other animals.

ECOSYSTEM: A community of living organisms and their environment interacting as a system.

EXOSKELETON: Meaning "outside skeleton," it is the hard outer body of some animals.

FILTER FEEDING: The process of straining suspended nutrients and food particles out of water for consumption.

GENES: Hereditary information passed from a parent animal to its offspring, resulting in functional characteristics.

HIERARCHY: The rank of animals within a group, including leaders and followers.

INCISOR: A sharp-edged tooth adapted for cutting.

INCUBATION: The process of keeping eggs warm until they hatch.

MILLENNIA: Periods of 1,000 years, each called a millennium.

MONOTREME: A type of mammal that lays eggs.

NACRE: The hard, iridescent substance that coats the inside of a mollusk's shell as it grows.

NEUROTOXIN: A chemical that affects the nerves and how the mind communicates with the body.

NOCTURNAL: Awake and active during the night and asleep during the day.

OBLIGATE: Meaning "by necessity," it is a biological term identifying characteristics necessary for an animal's survival.

PARASITE: An organism that lives in, on, or with another animal (called a host), surviving at the host animal's expense.

PASSERINE: Any bird of the order Passeriformes (more than half of all bird species), recognizable by the arrangement of their toes, which facilitates perching.

PHOTOPHORE: A bioluminescent organ, found on various marine animals.

PHOTOSYNTHESIS: The process through which green plants use sunlight to transform carbon dioxide and water into food.

PIGMENT: A natural coloring material found in plant and animal tissue.

POD: A school of marine mammals, such as seals, whales, or dolphins.

PREDATOR: An animal that hunts and kills other animals for its food.

PRIMATE: A member of the most highly developed order of animals, including monkeys, apes, and humans.

ROOKERY: A breeding place for birds and other animals.

SOLITARY: Living alone (or with a single mate) instead of in colonies or groups.

SYMBIOSIS: A mutually beneficial relationship between two organisms in an environment.

VERTEBRATE: An animal that has a backbone or spine.

ZOOLOGIST: One who studies animals (zoology).

INDEX

wandering spiders of Brazil, 39
spiny anteaters, 153, 154–55
sponges, 112–13
squid, 141
squirrels, 74
stingrays, 4
stonefish, 22–23
symbiotic relationships, 117

T

tapeworms, 18
tarantula hawk wasps, 96–97
tarantulas, 38
Texas, prairie dog town in, 45
tigers, 122
toads, 98–99
tortoises, 94
Tui Malila, 94
turkeys, 145
turtles, 14–17, 35

U

unicorns, 86

V

vampire bats, 150–51
vultures, 68–69, 142–43

W

wandering spiders of Brazil, 39
wasps, 96–97
whales, 126–27, 136–37
whale sharks, 28–29
white rhinos, 85
wolves, 80–81, 88–89, 122
worms, 18–19